Instant Slic3r

Unravel the mysteries behind taking a virtual model
and turning it into a physical object

David Michael Moore

PUBLISHING

BIRMINGHAM - MUMBAI

Instant Slic3r

First published: September 2013

Production Reference: 1240913

Published by Packt Publishing Ltd.
Livery Place
35 Livery Street
Birmingham B3 2PB, UK.

ISBN 978-1-78328-497-9

www.packtpub.com

Credits

Author
David Michael Moore

Reviewer
Niccolò Gallarati

Acquisition Editor
Joanne Fitzpatrick

Commissioning Editor
Shaon Basu

Technical Editors
Dennis John

Pramod Kumavat

Project Coordinator
Michelle Quadros

Proofreader
Jenny Blake

Production Coordinator
Nitesh Thakur

Cover Work
Nitesh Thakur

Cover Image
Valentina Dsilva

About the Author

David Michael Moore has been a lifelong maker. Starting at an early age taking apart his parents' alarm clocks, he has always been curious about how things work, and how they are put together. This drive was cemented in the seventh grade when he had a wood and metal shop.

A developer and designer by trade, David has been working with software for years. The current explosion of making rekindled his love of the physical act of making. He is often found in his workshop or in the basement working with wood, metal, plaster, plastic, and electronics, or musing about the act of making on `http://vandermore.com`.

He hopes to pass on his desire for making to his two daughters, so that their making spirit isn't overwhelmed by the consumer side of life.

I would like to thank my wife, Erin, for being so supportive of me in my building of things. I would also like to thank my parents, my grandfather Baw Baw, and my uncles, for giving me the drive to create and showing me that taking things apart can give me more parts for making new things.

About the Reviewer

Niccolò Gallarati developed his interest for technology since his childhood, when he learned how to use a screwdriver to tear everything electronic apart, much to the dismay of his parents. He graduated with a bachelor's degree in Communication Sciences and Technologies at IULM University, Milan, Italy. He is now a self-learned web developer, with a flair for digital marketing and friendly user interfaces. He has many years of experience in Web programming, IT hardware troubleshooting and maintenance, bug hunting, and customer support.

www.PacktPub.com

Support files, eBooks, discount offers and more

You might want to visit www.PacktPub.com for support files and downloads related to your book.

Did you know that Packt offers eBook versions of every book published, with PDF and ePub files available? You can upgrade to the eBook version at www.PacktPub.com and as a print book customer, you are entitled to a discount on the eBook copy. Get in touch with us at service@packtpub.com for more details.

At www.PacktPub.com, you can also read a collection of free technical articles, sign up for a range of free newsletters and receive exclusive discounts and offers on Packt books and eBooks.

http://PacktLib.PacktPub.com

Do you need instant solutions to your IT questions? PacktLib is Packt's online digital book library. Here, you can access, read and search across Packt's entire library of books.

Why Subscribe?

- ▶ Fully searchable across every book published by Packt
- ▶ Copy and paste, print and bookmark content
- ▶ On demand and accessible via web browser

Free Access for Packt account holders

If you have an account with Packt at www.PacktPub.com, you can use this to access PacktLib today and view nine entirely free books. Simply use your login credentials for immediate access.

Table of Contents

Preface

Slic3r, what is it? Why do we want to use it?

Slic3r is a part of a suite of software that can be used with a 3D printer to print objects. Its job is to take the three dimensional model that we want to print, and put it into a format that the printer firmware can understand so that it can print the object out for us.

Slic3r is a powerful tool that we can use to refine our prints without altering our model in any way. Settings in Slic3r can be adjusted so that our printer can produce strong parts for use in mechanical situations, or it can allow our printer to produce light and finely detailed objects that are purely decorative.

Mastery of Slic3r is crucial to creating good 3D prints from our printer, and this book strives to teach the knowledge and techniques required to fully take advantage of it.

What this book covers

Getting and installing Slic3r (Must know), covers how to get Slic3r and install it on your system. It covers getting the latest software, older versions, installing from source, and even installing on the Raspberry Pi.

Calibrating Slic3r to your printer (Must know), covers the basic setup of 3D printers going through Slic3r's configuration wizard, and printing your first object. It also goes through how to make different configurations for printers and different objects on the same printer.

Using Slic3r with other printer software (Should know), goes over how to install and use Slic3r with some of the most popular 3D printing software available. Also, it explains how Slic3r fits into the printing process and how you can use it standalone.

Layer height, fill settings, and perimeters in our objects (Should know), will talk about some of the most important settings for printing your objects. It delves into how each setting works, and how changing it will affect your final printed object.

Print speed, cooling, support material, and more... (Should know), acknowledges that printing great objects is wonderful; however waiting for them can be difficult. Having the model come out warped or sagging is also disappointing. Hence this recipe goes over how to speed up printing and how cooling and adding support material can help produce great prints faster.

Troubleshooting your prints (Should know), guides you through how to troubleshoot your prints, teaching you the skill of troubleshooting, in addition to giving you answers to possible problems.

Running Slic3r from the command line (Become an expert), acknowledges that Slic3r is powerful, even more powerful than you realize. Running from the command line can give you the ability to integrate Slic3r into other scripts or software, even your own printing suite. This recipe goes over the functionality that you can use when using Slic3r from the command line.

The basics of G-code (Should know), sheds light on what is G-code and what it does. The instructions here guide you through an actual model's G-code, and how it is used by the printer to make your prints. It also gives you the tools to understand G-code for use in the next recipe.

Post processing with Slic3r (Become an expert), shows you how to use Slic3r to run post-processing scripts on Slic3r's output to do calculations on cost of materials, cleaning up models, and more.

What you need for this book

In order to use this book, you'll need a computer. Windows, Mac, or Linux are all capable of running Slic3r. A Raspberry Pi running Raspbian will also run Slic3r, though having a laptop or desktop for learning Slic3r on will be preferable.

You will also need a copy of Slic3r compatible with your operating system. Downloads for Slic3r can be found at `http://slic3r.org`. We also go over getting and installing Slic3r in the first recipe *Getting and installing Slic3r (Must know)*.

You'll need a 3D printer if you want to actually print objects, and you will also need printing software for your OS and 3D printer. Those can be found at your printer's website.

That's all!

Who this book is for

This book is for those starting out with 3D printing and 3D printing software. It's meant to help people understand how Slic3r works and how it fits into the 3D printing tool chain.

Slicers are an integral part of 3D printing, and this book strives to teach people how Slic3r does what it does, and how they can tune it to make the best 3D prints possible for their printer.

Conventions

In this book, you will find a number of styles of text that distinguish between different kinds of information. Here are some examples of these styles, and an explanation of their meaning.

Code words in text are shown as follows: "You can click on the file link to download the Slic3r software. The filename starts with `slic3r-osx-` and ends in `.dmg`."

A block of code is set as follows:

```
M109 S200 ; wait for temperature to be reached
G90 ; use absolute coordinates
G92 E0 ; reset extrusion distance
M82 ; use absolute distances for extrusion
G1 F1800.000 E-1.00000 ; retract
```

When we wish to draw your attention to a particular part of a code block, the relevant lines or items are set in bold:

```
M109 S200 ; wait for temperature to be reached
G90 ; use absolute coordinates
G92 E0 ; reset extrusion distance
M82 ; use absolute distances for extrusion
G1 F1800.000 E-1.00000 ; retract
```

Any command-line input or output is written as follows:

```
sudo apt-get install libextutils-cbuilder-perl
slic3r-console.exe.
```

New terms and **important words** are shown in bold. Words that you see on the screen, in menus or dialog boxes for example, appear in the text like this: "We can hit the **Next** button after reading the welcome message to get started with the configuration."

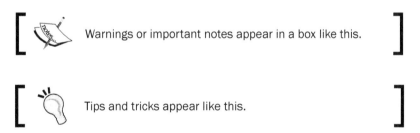

> Warnings or important notes appear in a box like this.

> Tips and tricks appear like this.

Reader feedback

Feedback from our readers is always welcome. Let us know what you think about this book—what you liked or may have disliked. Reader feedback is important for us to develop titles that you really get the most out of. To send us general feedback, simply send an e-mail to feedback@packtpub.com, and mention the book title via the subject of your message. If there is a topic that you have expertise in and you are interested in either writing or contributing to a book, see our author guide on www.packtpub.com/authors.

Customer support

Now that you are the proud owner of a Packt book, we have a number of things to help you to get the most from your purchase.

Errata

Although we have taken every care to ensure the accuracy of our content, mistakes do happen. If you find a mistake in one of our books—maybe a mistake in the text or the code—we would be grateful if you would report this to us. By doing so, you can save other readers from frustration and help us improve subsequent versions of this book. If you find any errata, please report them by visiting http://www.packtpub.com/submit-errata, selecting your book, clicking on the **errata submission form** link, and entering the details of your errata. Once your errata are verified, your submission will be accepted and the errata will be uploaded on our website, or added to any list of existing errata, under the Errata section of that title. Any existing errata can be viewed by selecting your title from http://www.packtpub.com/support.

Piracy

Piracy of copyright material on the Internet is an ongoing problem across all media. At Packt, we take the protection of our copyright and licenses very seriously. If you come across any illegal copies of our works, in any form, on the Internet, please provide us with the location address or website name immediately so that we can pursue a remedy.

Please contact us at copyright@packtpub.com with a link to the suspected pirated material.

We appreciate your help in protecting our authors, and our ability to bring you valuable content.

Questions

You can contact us at questions@packtpub.com if you are having a problem with any aspect of the book, and we will do our best to address it.

Instant Slic3r

Welcome to *Instant Slic3r*. So you've decided to try out Slic3r for your 3D printing process. Maybe you chose it because it could print support material. Perhaps you chose it for its ability to lay out a whole plate of objects while still allowing you to print only one.

You may also like how you can use either a graphical user interface (GUI) or the command line to run Slic3r. You might even be using Slic3r already in one of several software packages, such as Pronterface, ReplicatorG, or Repetier-Host, and want to know more about Slic3r, or want to upgrade the version that came with your software package.

Getting and installing Slic3r (Must know)

In order for us to use Slic3r, first we need to get it, and this is fairly simple. This recipe will cover the different platforms that Slic3r is available on (Mac OS X, Windows, Linux, and Raspberry Pi). It will also cover the steps for getting and installing the stable release version for each platform, and how to get older versions if you need them.

Getting ready

Slic3r is undergoing lots of development. This recipe will talk about how to get the latest stable release. While you can get the latest release if you build from the source, we're going to talk about getting the release built here, in this recipe, because it will be the most stable. If you are interested in building from the source, we will cover that at the end of this recipe.

How to do it...

As we talked about earlier, we are getting the release version.

1. Navigate to `http://www.slic3r.org` and select the **Download** link at the top of the page. You can also go directly to the download page at `http://www.slic3r.org/download`.

2. Select the operating system that you use. Slic3r is available for Mac OS X, Windows (32 bit and 64 bit), along with Linux (also both 32 bit and 64 bit). The Linux versions that run on Raspberry Pi need some special attention and we will cover installing that separately when we get to installing from the source. Once you click on the icon for your operating system, it may be a bit confusing at first glance to chose which file to download. For all operating systems, the link icon takes you to a page that has a folder labeled `old`, and one or more file links.

For us, the choice of Mac OS X here is simple. You can click on the file link to download the Slic3r software. The filename starts with `slic3r-osx-` and ends in `.dmg`. The text in the middle is the version number of the software, but we don't need to worry about that right now, since we just want the latest build.

For Windows, there will be two choices:

> ▸ For 64 bit machines, download the file that starts with `slic3r-mswin-x64` and ends with `.zip`
> ▸ For 32 bit machines, click on the file that starts with `slic3r-mswin-x86` and ends with `.zip`

For Linux machines there are also two choices (one for 32 bit and one for 64 bit like the Windows version):

> ▸ For 64 bit Linux versions, get the file that starts with `slic3r-linux-x86_64` and ends with `.tar.gz`
> ▸ For 32 bit Linux machines, download the file that has `slic3r-linux` without the `_64` term, also ending in `.tar.gz`

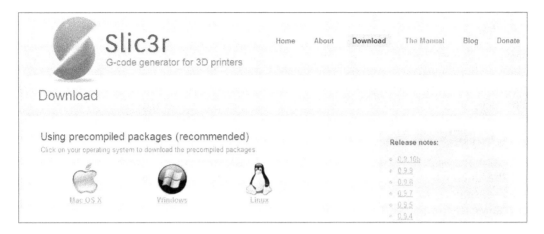

Once you have the software downloaded, it's time to put it where we want it. There's no actual installation, as it is a standalone program.

- ▸ **Mac OS X**: The .dmg file can be installed just like any other program on Mac. Double-click on it and drag the content of the opened folder into the Applications folder of your drive.

- ▸ **Windows and Linux**: Uncompress the .zip or tar.gz file and place the Slic3r folder in a convenient location on your system. On Windows, I usually put it on C:\Slic3r, so I can find it easily.

Now you can launch Slic3r as you would any other program on your OS.

How it works...

Slic3r is built on the Perl programming language with some parts written in C++. Perl is known for its ability to parse files in a quick and efficient manner, and is one of the reasons why Slic3r is so fast at slicing STL and other files.

It is also a language that is known for allowing developers to work quickly, though it is also notoriously hard to read for people not familiar with the language.

There's more...

Slic3r is undergoing constant development. At the time of writing, there have been incremental versions every two to three months. The primary developer of Slic3r, Alessandro Ranellucci, is constantly making improvements in speed and adding new features. He is assisted by several other developers and the open source community, comprising of you and me.

Getting older builds

If, for some reason, you need an older version of the software, we can get that too. Just go into the "old" folder of the required operating system, and select the version that you want. The release notes for each version are on the download page of Slic3r.org, where you originally chose your operating system.

> Given that Slic3r isn't installed on Windows or Linux machines, we can even run different versions of Slic3r on the same machine by keeping the versions in separate folders. This is because Slic3r is a standalone program and doesn't need to be installed into the operating system on which we will be running it.

Running from source code

Slic3r's source code can be found on GitHub.com (https://github.com/alexrj/Slic3r is the original repository), and it is licensed under the GNU Affero General Public License, Version 3, which means that we can look at the source code, modify it, and even create products out of it, as long as we post the modified source code we made (see the license for full details).

What does this mean for us? Well, it means that we can build Slic3r from the source. If you want to have the most bleeding edge version of Slic3r—because it fixes an issue you have with the current release build, or maybe you just want to have the newest and shiniest version of the software—you can get the source code and build it yourself. You might even have an idea for an improvement to Slic3r and want to contribute. All of these are valid reasons why we want to look at building from the source code.

The instructions for building from source for each system are located on the download page of Slic3r.org. You will require a version of Perl on your system to build Slic3r; the instructions for it and getting any of its other dependencies are in each OS's instruction.

Installing on Raspberry Pi

Raspberry Pi is a small computer (about the width and height of a credit card) that costs about $35 and requires very little power to run. People have been wanting to use it with their 3D printers to make their setup smaller and less dependent on a desktop or laptop to run.

The Raspberry Pi is an ARM-based computer, and has very little processing power and RAM. So while it has the benefits of portability, it will take longer to slice our objects than it would on another machine.

At the time of writing, Slic3r has been installed and runs on a Raspberry Pi using the Raspbian operating system. You might hear it called a **distro** by some, because it is a distribution of Linux made for Raspberry Pi. The instructions for installing it are almost the same as the installation for Linux, but with a few changes. The following commands must all be run from the command line or terminal window:

1. Go to `https://github.com/alexrj/Slic3r/wiki/Running-Slic3r-from-git-on-GNU-Linux` and follow the **Install dependencies through the package manager** instructions.

2. Before moving on to **Get Slic3r**, we will need to install a few extra dependencies, because Raspbian does not install everything that a full-sized Linux install would. The following three dependencies need to be installed:

   ❏ `sudo apt-get install libextutils-cbuilder-perl`

   ❏ `sudo apt-get install gcc-4.7`

   ❏ `sudo apt-get install g++-4.7`

3. We can now proceed with the rest of the instructions on the page, starting with **Get Slic3r**.

4. If you run into any issues, the `build.log` file will tell you what went wrong and whether any other dependencies need to be installed.

 The `build.log` file is located at `~/.cpanm/build.log`.

Calibrating Slic3r to your printer (Must know)

In order to get the very best prints from your 3D printer, you have to calibrate Slic3r to your specific printer. Each 3D printer brand will have its own calibration settings; even printers in the same brand will have differences. If you have built your own 3D printer, great! But it's even more important for us to calibrate Slic3r to your printer to get the very best prints out of it.

Getting ready

The first thing we need to make sure is that the printer, which we will be calibrating, is set up properly and will be able to produce a good print on its own. What this means is that we need to make sure of the following:

- The frame is sturdy, with no wobble, and its alignment is true.
- All of the belts, if it has any, are taut.
- The filament comes freely from its spool or dispenser. If it doesn't come easily, it can cause too much tension on the extruder, which leads to bad prints and possible extruder damage.
- The print bed is level in relation to the extruder(s). Refer to your printer setup for exact information on how to do this.
- If you built the printer we are using, make sure that the electricity supply to the stepper motors is set correctly.
- All of your firmware settings for your printer are correct. If the firmware isn't set properly for our extruder or axis steppers, that will also cause bad prints.

The bottom line for this is to make sure our printer itself is calibrated and functional before adding something else to calibrate. If the printer isn't calibrated correctly, we will have a hard or impossible time calibrating Slic3r to produce good prints.

How to do it...

While it is possible to configure Slic3r using the command line, the developers of Slic3r have made things easier for us—the new and experienced 3D printer owners. They've produced a **Configuration Wizard** to help get Slic3r set up and ready for printing our first print easily.

Let us see what steps we need to follow for setting the physical printer properties:

1. Starting the **Configuration Wizard**:

Starting our installation

1. When you start Slic3r, the **Configuration Wizard** is located under the **Help** menu.

2. We can hit the **Next** button after reading the welcome message to get started with the configuration.

2. Setting the firmware type:

1. The next step is selecting your firmware type. If you don't see the type of printer you have in the drop-down box, you will need to contact the supplier.

The **firmware** is the software that is burned onto the chip (usually ATMega) of the board that controls your printer. When new firmware are released, Slic3r gets updated with them. So if you update your firmware, you should be able to run the wizard again to update your configuration.

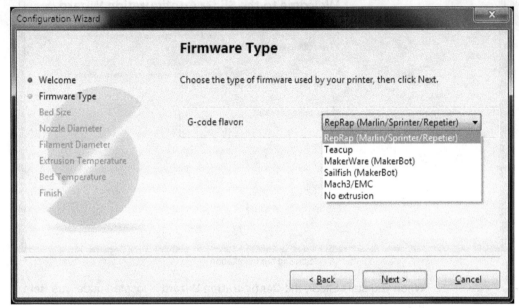

Picking the firmware type

3. The next step is to set the bed size:

   Setting the bed size is important, because that is what makes sure your prints can fit on your printer. This step is easy, but critical.

   1. The place to start measurements is the lower-left corner of the bed where the nozzle rests at its home position (0, 0).

   2. Measuring from that point to the far right position of where the extruder can travel safely will be your X value in millimeters.

   3. Measuring from (0,0) away from you on the bed as far as the extruder can move in that direction will give you the Y value in millimeters.

4. We need to make sure that in taking those measurements the extruder doesn't hit any other part of the machine as it travels. If it does, the bed size should be smaller.

5. Firmware settings that configure end-stop locations may also limit the bed size, so we need to check those in the firmware as well if the print is not printing to what we think is the full size.

Setting the bed size

4. Setting the nozzle diameter:

    Common values for most printer nozzles now is 3.5mm or 5mm. If you don't know the size, measure it carefully. This can be difficult because the hole is very small.

1. If you have a hard time measuring it, the suggestion on the Slic3r site is a good one. Slowly and carefully extrude (1mm/s) some filament and measure the thickness of the extruded plastic. We will need to use our printing software to do this, because Slic3r doesn't directly control the printer. This will give us an accurate measurement and also takes thermal swelling of the extruder nozzle into account. If you feel ambitious, or want extra-precise detail, using this on a known nozzle size can be a good idea.

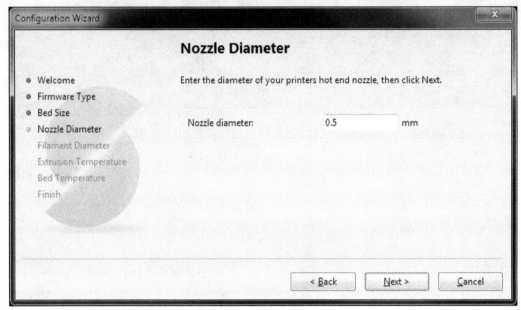

Assigning the nozzle diameter

5. Filament diameter

A little known fact among budding 3D printing enthusiasts is that filament sizes are actually the ideal filament size. In order to know how much plastic is pushed through the extruder, we need to have a more accurate gauge of the filament size.

1. We need to measure the filament in several places to get an average of the thickness. A digital caliper is good for taking measurements along several lengths of our filament.

2. We will then take the average of those measurements and input that into the wizard's filament diameter.

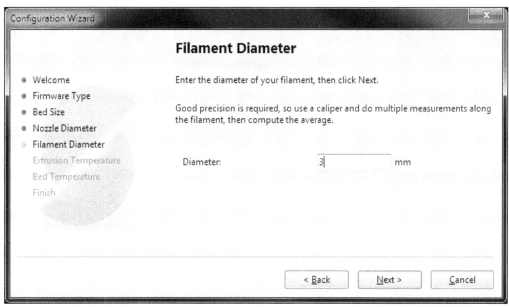

Setting the filament diameter – remember to take the average of our measurements

6. Setting the extrusion temperature:

Now we come to one of the two settings that we will be tweaking throughout our further setup process. The first setting is the extrusion temperature, which specifies how hot the extruder nozzle will get in order to melt the plastic and get it flowing through the nozzle.

1. The wizard gives the temperature ranges for both PLA and ABS plastic. Different colors of plastic will affect the temperature because the dye used can affect the chemical makeup, and thus the melting temperatures of the plastic.

2. For now, we will leave this setting at 200° C and adjust it later.

3. If the printing software we will be using has a temperature control, we should set this value to 0 and let the printer software handle the extrusion temperature.

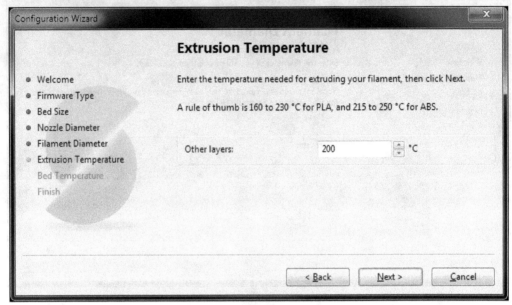

Setting the extrusion temperature

7. Setting the bed temperature:

When the plastic is melted, it remains sticky, but when it cools, the stickiness goes away. So when we print, we want to have a bed that the plastic will stick to.

1. Not all printers have a heated bed, but if we do, we should set this to either 60° C for PLA plastic or 110° C for ABS plastic.

2. This setting is also one of those we will tweak as we do our test prints, and we learn how our printer behaves.

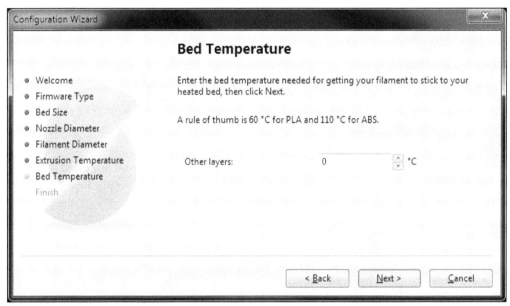

Setting the bed temperature

Done! We're ready to check out Slic3r and print our first print to test our printer.

Finishing the installation

How it works...

Slic3r needs these steps done in order to produce good prints. Letting Slic3r know our printer's specifications means that when it slices models for printing, they will be in a scale that matches our printer.

Making sure our printer is solid, with no wobbling or shaking, will let our printer not mar or destroy the object we are trying to print. If we don't have these things set correctly, the print could be misshapen, the print nozzle could hit the print bed, or worse.

There's more...

Low cost, home 3D printing is a new field. Don't be discouraged if our first few prints aren't perfect. Here we will look at some good sample models to do test prints with, saving multiple configurations to help us try and dial in the quality of our printer.

Testing the settings and printing our first model

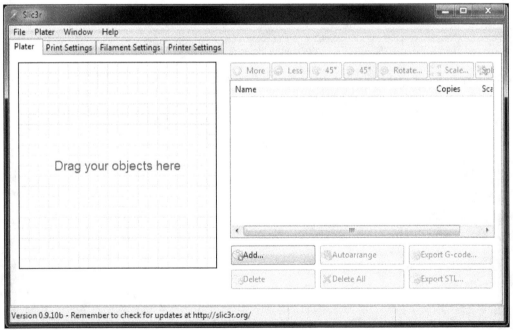

The Slic3r interface

So we've calibrated our printer hardware and have run through the Configuration Wizard. Now, we print! Okay, not yet, we don't have a model to print.

Getting a model isn't hard at all. People have been making models for 3D printers like ours for a while now. One good site is **Thingiverse** (`http://www.thingiverse.com`). While any model there could be printed, for our first print, we would want to start off small.

Why small? We don't want to waste plastic, and more importantly, time, on a print that might not come out right. There are two models I suggest: **Snake** by Zomboe (`http://www.thingiverse.com/thing:4743`), and **Torture Test** by MAKE (`http://www.thingiverse.com/thing:33902`). Both are smaller and they test our printer's capabilities.

If we are setting up this printer for the first time along with setting up Slic3r, another good model would be the 20mm Cube by Engineglue (`http://www.thingiverse.com/thing:34553`). By printing this, and stopping the print before it has started printing the top, will allow us to measure its wall thickness, see how true our x and y axis are, and even calibrate our flow rate.

Slic3r can use several different file types. The ones at Thingiverse are almost always the first and most accepted 3D printing format: **STL**. It stands for **StereoLithography**, which is another form of 3D printing that is becoming more available to hobbyist 3D printers.

The other two formats are **Wavefront OBJ**, and **Additive Manufacturing File Format** (**AMF**). AMF is actually now a standard for 3D printing, because it can do things STL files can't, such as describing colors and materials in the modeling file. It's newer and still hasn't caught on as much as the de facto standard of STL files.

Now that we've got a model, either from a third party, or the one that we have build ourselves, we can set up our first print.

In the Slic3r GUI, the first tab is called **Plater**. Plater allows us to load and place objects to be printed. There are a couple of nice things about Plater. One, we can just drag-and-drop objects into it from our desktop. Two, we can load in more than one object to print and arrange them on the print area so we don't have to have multiple prints for a bunch of smaller objects.

So let's go ahead and drag a model in, or use the **Add...** button on the same tab window. Once it's loaded, several other option buttons will become enabled. We are going to leave those alone for now, as we just want to print the model.

Now, we print!

Go ahead and hit **Export G-code...** to slice our model and use your printer software to print the object. If you are using printer software that has Slic3r built in, print using its instructions.

Saving our configuration

So we've made our initial configuration and want to make some changes. We might have another 3D printer we want to print from; what do we do to save this configuration? By default, Slic3r saves our original settings from when we went through the Configuration Wizard. We want to save a copy of it though, so we can get back to it later if it's better than the changes we make. Of course, when we have our settings dialed in, we'll also want to save that configuration as a backup, in case something happens to the one that is loaded.

Saving a single configuration is easy. Navigate to **File | Export Config...**. It will bring up a Save dialog with the default name of `config.ini`. We should rename it to something that is easier to remember and associated with the printer. A good format to use would be `config_PRINTER_DATE.ini`, so we know what printer the config is for and what date it was saved. If it's one we want to really remember, some additional information can be put into the filename.

To load in the configuration file later, it's as simple as navigating to **File | Load Config...** and then selecting the configuration we want.

This is great for one, or even a few, configurations. But what happens if you want to print in PLA and ABS, have a model that has special print settings for, or even have a few printers? It would be a pain to keep importing configurations over and over. That's where Slic3r profiles come in.

Slic3r profiles

We've already created a Slic3r profile, but it's hidden from us right now. If you feel comfortable enough delving into the expert level of Slic3r, the following is how we can set up profiles.

1. Navigate to **File | Preferences...**, and in the **Mode:** dropdown, select **Expert**. Hit **OK** and Slic3r will tell you that you have to restart Slic3r to get to the Expert settings. Let's do that now.

2. Close Slic3r and then restart it. The first thing we notice is a new row of drop-down menus on the **Plater** tab.

3. Open the **Printer Settings** tab and you'll see a new column on the left-hand side with a dropdown and below it three items that you can select: **General**, **Custom G-code**, and **Extruder 1**. To create our first profile, hit the disk icon next to the drop-down menu, and in the pop up, input a name for the profile that makes sense and is easy to understand later.

We've saved our first profile. We can now use this profile as a base for tweaking settings, or for setting up a new printer. If by chance we want to get rid of a profile, clicking on the red delete icon next to the save icon while the profile is loaded will allow us to delete the profile. As a safety, there is always a `default-` profile that can't be deleted that we can always go back to.

Going to the **Print Settings** tab, and the **Filament Settings** tab, we can see that we can also save profiles there. This is really useful, as we can then mix and match all three profiles on the **Plater** tab at the bottom where those three new dropdowns showed up. So now we can have one **Printer Profile**, and can change our **Filament Profiles** if we change spools of filament to another color or from one plastic type to another; all without loading in custom configuration files.

Using Slic3r with other printer software (Should know)

So we've printed our test pieces and done a little fine tuning. Since Slic3r is updating constantly, we'll eventually want to update it and have our printer software use the new version. We'll look at how to update Slic3r for three of the most popular printer software packages: Printrun, Repetier-Host, and Replicator-G.

 At the time of this book's writing, the release version of Slic3r is 0.9.10b. There is a bug in the console version that causes an error when slicing. This does not occur in 0.9.9, and is fixed for the next version in the repository. So if you have issues with any of these printers, you can slice with the Slic3r GUI, or you can install a different version of Slic3r instead of 0.9.10b.

Getting ready

In the *Calibrating Slic3r to your printer (Must know)* recipe, we went over how to set up Slic3r and testing a print. Now we want to update Slic3r, or change to a different printing software, but still use Slic3r for slicing our models to print.

Most printing software that comes with Slic3r will release an update just after Slic3r releases a new build. So the easiest way to update is to just wait for one.

What if we want a feature *now* though? What if we've edited the Slic3r code ourselves and want to test it before submitting a pull request to the Slic3r repository? The process for installing a new version of Slic3r in most printer software is quick, once you know how.

How to do it...

The instructions here are based on the Windows version of Slic3r. Most, however, can be be used with Mac and Linux installs with little or no changes.

For those of us with the Printrun suite of software, we'll the next set of instructions to install or upgrade Slic3r.

Printrun is actually a collection of software: Pronterface, Prontserve, Pronsole, and Printcore. Pronterface is the actual printing software that we need to integrate Slic3r with.

1. Download the version of Slic3r that we want to install and unzip it. We'll want these files in a moment.

Name	Date modified	Type	Size
bin	6/15/2013 12:33 PM	File folder	
cpfworkrt	7/12/2013 11:49 AM	File folder	
dll	7/12/2013 11:49 AM	File folder	
lib	7/12/2013 11:49 AM	File folder	
res	7/12/2013 11:49 AM	File folder	
slic3r.exe	6/15/2013 12:33 PM	Application	576 KB
slic3r-console.exe	6/15/2013 12:33 PM	Application	576 KB

Slic3r files to be copied

2. Locate the install directory for Printrun. As Printrun on Windows is not installed, the location of this directory is where you originally unzipped the software to.

3. Inside the Printrun directory, there is a `Slic3r` directory.

4. Copy the files from the `Slic3r` directory that we downloaded, and paste them into this directory.

5. Once that is done, the new version Slic3r is ready to be used by Printrun for slicing.

For more information on Printrun, including more details on how Slic3r can be integrated into Printrun's settings, head over to the Printrun repository at `https://github.com/kliment/Printrun`.

Another popular printing software is **Repetier-Host**. Repetier-Host comes with Slic3r, so updating it is quite easy.

1. Select the **Slicer** tab in Repetier-Host, and click on the **Setup** button in the **Slic3r** section:

The Slicer tab in Repetier-Host

2. In the dialog that comes up, we can then select the **Slic3r Configuration Directory**. If we leave it blank, Repetier-Host will use it's default path:

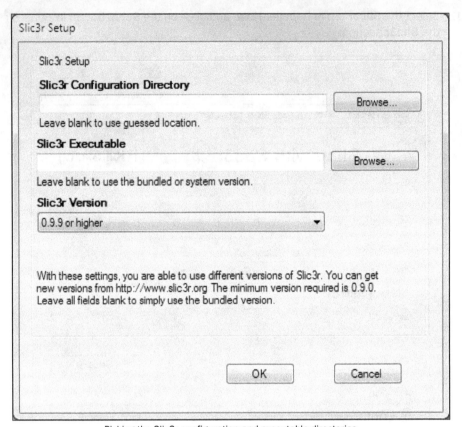

Picking the Slic3r configuration and executable directories

3. Then we need to mention the directory where the new version of Slic3r is located. As the dialog says, leaving that section blank will tell Repetier-Host to use the default version of Slic3r that is bundled with Repetier-Host.

4. After we click on **OK**, Repetier-Host is ready to use the new version of Slic3r we installed.

 The minimum version of Slic3r that Repetier-Host uses is 0.9.0.

Replicator-G is what comes with MakerBot, so its popularity has been tied to the popularity of the MakerBot itself.

Replicator-G comes with Skeinforge installed by default, so we need to make some changes to get it to use Slic3r. It isn't as easy to switch as Repetier-Host is, but it's only a little more difficult than Printrun. So if you aren't comfortable with overwriting the previous version of Slic3r, skip to the *There's more...* section for another way to use different versions of Slic3r with Replicator-G.

1. After downloading the version of Slic3r you want, install it and open the directory you chose for the install.
2. Select all of the files inside the Slic3r folder, and copy them. Moving them is fine, but I prefer having a standalone copy of Slic3r as well.
3. On Windows, there will be a `ReplicatorG` directory inside the user directory.
4. Navigate to `ReplicatorG\replicatorg-0040\skein_engines\slic3r_engines\windows`.
5. Now we paste (or move) the files from the Slic3r directory into the now open directory.

This will change out Slic3r for Replicator-G. The settings for Replicator-G are still experimental, so some tweaking will be needed to get really good prints.

To use Slic3r with Replicator-G, navigate to **GCode | GCode Generator | Slic3r 0.X - Experimental**.

How it works...

We all have our own favorite things we use. Printing software is no different. We've decided to either give Slic3r a try on our favorite software, or try out different printer software. Either way, we need to know how to get the software to talk to each other.

Just like an inkjet or laser printer, a 3D printer has to get a file from the computer in a certain format in order to print. This is usually handled by printer drivers for that particular printer.

Personal 3D printing isn't quite to that stage yet, so we need to provide the printer with input that it can understand. You can think of Slic3r as part of the Print Settings dialog that would normally come up before printing on a paper printer. The printer software is a combination of the printer driver and the rest of the options in the Print Settings window.

There's more...

Not every 3D printing software will take Slic3r as its slicing software. There are still a few ways we can use Slic3r on our favorite printer software.

Other printer software

While we can't cover every printer software out there, there are ways to get Slic3r into your tool chain if you use something different. Most printer software will take G-code files directly and print those.

Some people decide to actually use Slic3r outside of their printing software. They load the model up in Slic3r first and slice it, then load the resulting G-code file into their printing software to print.

There are more 3D printing software packages being developed even now. Those might not be as easy to update with Slic3r, or might not even allow alternate slicing programs. So using Slic3r as a standalone program to slice your models first and then using the printer software may be the route to go in some cases.

Layer height, fill settings, and perimeters in our objects (Should know)

So we've delved into getting and installing Slic3r, doing our initial printer calibration, printing our first print, and using Slic3r with other printer software. Where do we go from here? Well, right now our prints aren't the best in the world, there are some settings in Slic3r that could help make them better.

Getting ready

Open up Slic3r and go to the **Print Settings** tab. We're staying in the **Simple** mode for now, because it's easier to track the changes we make to the changes in our final print.

 A good thing to do when making setting changes is to only make one change at a time. This is so that if something goes wrong, or right, we know exactly what change did it.

How to do it...

The **Print Settings** section is where a lot of changes will happen as we print. Let's go down the list of options in this section so we know what they are and why we might want to change them, sometimes from print to print.

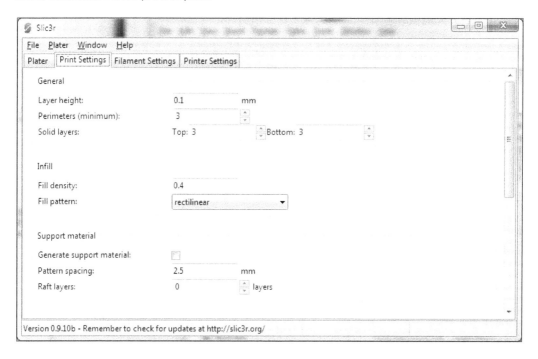

1. First up is **Layer height** option. The default layer height of 0.4mm is ok, assuming that we have a 0.5mm nozzle. So we can leave that for now.
   - If our nozzle is more than 0.5mm though, we will have a lot of squeeze out of our filament. So if our nozzle is larger, increase the size of the layer. 80 percent of the nozzle diameter is a good rule of thumb.
   - This also means that if we have a nozzle less than 0.5mm, we can make our layer height default smaller. Again, 80 percent of the nozzle diameter is a good starting place.

2. Depending on our object we are printing, the **Perimeters (minimum)** setting of **3** is good.

   If there are gaps in the walls, especially of sloped surfaces, increasing the number of perimeters is something to try.

3. Next, **Solid layers** is the setting of how many layers Slic3r will tell the printer to fill completely at the top and the bottom of the print.

   - For the bottom layers, this will give the object a stable base that is less prone to warping.

   - For the top, the default of **3** layers is based on the extruded filament width, and how much coverage the filament will give as it gets to the top of the object.

4. For the **Infill** settings, a value of **0.15** for **Fill density** should stay, but change **Fill pattern** to **honeycomb**. It's a bit slower, but more stable.

   This is how the inner part of the object is filled with plastic. Since filling the entire object uses a lot of plastic, and isn't needed, we set the infill settings.

How it works...

Layer height, infill settings, perimeters, what does it all mean? Let's look into those settings and what they stand for, in more detail.

Layer height

The layer height of the print means how thick each layer of plastic is deposited on the model. The thinner the layer, the smoother and more detailed the print can be.

We don't always want thin layers though. Some prints, such as for mechanical parts, or parts that will not be seen, can be done with thicker layer heights. If we're printing parts for a RepRap or another printer, the layer height can be thicker for the structural elements. It doesn't directly relate to the structural strength however. That would be covered in a moment when discussing the **Perimeters** and **Infill** settings.

For thicker layer heights, it's usually a good idea to have layers at or under your nozzle size. This is so the extruder will press the plastic into the layer below. If the layer height is higher, the plastic will have a chance to cool before touching the foundation layer, and also only have gravity to help weld the two layers together.

If we're printing objects for viewing, such as a statue or a decorative item, we'll usually want to go with thinner layer heights. This comes at the expense of printing speed, because the printer will now need to lay down more layers to complete the model. So finding a balance between looks and speed is something we will constantly juggle.

For very detailed objects, resolutions as low as 0.1mm have been achieved by some printers.

Perimeters

These make up the walls of the object. They are also important for adding stability to the object being printed. The Slic3r developers recommend a minimum of two perimeters for printing. Having at least two will help both the structure of the outside, and help to cover up imperfections in the print.

There is also a setting for solid layers. It is related to **Perimeters**, in that, it determines the number of solid layers at the top and the bottom of the print. The default setting for this is three perimeters.

For models that are not solid, set them with the **Infill** settings; having more than one top layer will help bridge any gaps in the model and will result in a better fill for the top of the model.

The default setting for Slic3r is for the three top and bottom layers to be solid. Depending on our model, and what we want to do with it, we can change this. Coming up is a hack for making hollow objects such as vases from normally solid objects.

Infill settings

Infill in our objects gives them stability. Too much infill, however, such as making our object solid, can not only cause printing issues, but also is a waste of plastic.

The **Fill Density** setting ranges from 0 to 1, with 0 being 0 percent, and 1 being 100 percent. The default setting for **Fill Density** is 40 percent, or 0.4 in the preference. This is a decent setting to start with, but for structural components, or ones that will depend on being rigid under stress, raising that up would be a good idea.

The developers suggest a minimum of 0.2 as the setting to support flat ceilings. Any lower, the top of your model is likely to sag inward.

The **Fill Pattern** is interesting. This setting is how Slic3r will tell our printer how to fill in the inside of our model. The **honeycomb** option is good for structure, but takes longer to print. The developers also recommend **rectilinear** and **line** for infill, but there are several others to choose from. A bit of experimentation will reveal what is best for what models we want to print.

There's more...

Settings can be more than just settings. More than just a tool for making nicer quality prints. We can use some settings to alter the objects themselves, to make changes to the objects, and have it come out as what we want without having to touch the modeling software.

Vases and other hollow objects

There are some interesting things you can do while printing models and changing these settings. For instance, if you set the **Infill Fill Density** to 0, and the **Top** setting of **Solid layers** to 0, you can make any object hollow with the top open.

We'll need to make sure the model can actually print this way, structurally. If it can, it is an interesting way to make custom vases or other open cupped objects. Having a higher setting on the **Perimeters (minimum)** will help some prints with this.

Print speed, cooling, support material, and more... (Should know)

In this recipe we will start to delve into the advanced settings of Slic3r. Now that we've had a few prints using Slic3r and tweaked the settings as far as we could to get the best prints possible, we'll be switching to the Expert mode. The Expert mode will allow us to fine tune our efforts and adjust things such as the speed of our printer and add support structures to give our model stability during printing.

As we have done in the past, we will be making one change at a time to see how it affects the quality of the print. We have been doing that, right? Getting those models in our hands faster is great, but having great models is even better (and more useful).

Getting ready

Sometimes the prints don't come out well as we would like them. This recipe will help us refine the objects that we print. So let's pull out our favorite torture test model file and let's get to work.

How to do it...

We'll now go through the steps to give us access to the more advanced settings. With access to these, we will be able to make better prints, faster, and more reliably than just using the basic settings we have been using.

Switching to the Expert mode:

1. Under **File | Preferences**, change the value of **Mode** to **Expert**.
2. Restart Slic3r for the changes to take effect.
3. When Slic3r is restarted, go to the **Print Settings** tab to see the changes.

Changing the Infill settings:

1. Go to the **Print Settings** tab.

2. Select **Infill** from the menu on the left.

3. Change the **Fill Density**.

   - If we have parts that need to take mechanical stresses, or should have more of a heft to them, we will increase the fill density.

   - If we have parts that need to be more hollow, or are more decorative, we might even go below the default 0.4 (40%) **Fill Density**.

4. Next we should change **Fill Pattern**. There are a variety of fill patterns for our infill. Earlier we chose **honeycomb**, which is a common choice for most people out there doing 3D printing. Feel free to try other styles though.

   The styles marked (slow) are both mathematically intense for the printer to interpret, and also tend to use more plastic when printing. Again, some models may benefit from this.

Changing Speed settings

1. In the left-hand side, click on **Speed**. Here we find a dizzying array of settings that we can work with to improve the print quality, while balancing that with improving the speed of the print. Look at the settings for **Speed**:

   - Inside it we can see settings similar to others that we have set before, only these have **mm/s** or % next to the values. This sets the speed of our extruder when the printer is printing different parts of our model.

   - Notice how the **First layer speed** is 30 percent of the print speed of the rest of the print.

   - The **Travel** for non-print moves is increased, because we don't need the precision to lay down the filament.

   - Once we have changed a setting, print something small so we can see how it affects both the print quality and the time it takes to print.

Changing the Skirt and Brim settings

1. Select **Skirt and brim** from the left-hand side menu inside the **Print Settings** tab.

   The skirt settings control the filament print that encircles our print. It is used most often to prime the print head and make sure that the extruder and bed are up to temperature. Having the bed be at the right temperature ensures that our model will stay put during the print. Having a skirt printed will show us before we start the model if the bed is at the proper temperature.

2.   Let's go ahead and change the value of **Brim width**, under **Brim**, for a print.

Brim width is a thin layer of plastic that will be extruded around the model. Just the first layer print of the model will have this brim. Unlike Skirt, Brim is actually connected to the model, and is used to help models adhere to the heated bed if they have small pieces at the bottom of the model.

Changing the Support material settings

1.   Select **Support material** from the left-hand side menu of **Print Settings**.

2.   Check the box for **Generate support material**. This will now print some plastic under the model where the model would have overhangs.

3.   **Overhang threshold** is the setting to adjust if our model has an overhang and needs more support material under it. We can also change it the other way if we know our model's overhang won't need support; this will speed up our print time as we don't have to print support material.

4.   We can also enforce support for the first several layers if we feel that a model needs it, even if it doesn't exceed the overhang threshold. Say we have a model that has trouble sticking to the bed. Increase the value of **Raft layers** by 1 or more to tell our printer to lay down layers of plastic before printing the model. This will help the model to not get warped, and continue to stick to the bed. Unfortunately, this also means that we need to clean off the support material and raft after the print is done.

5.   The remaining options for support material and raft should be self-explanatory:

   ❑   **Pattern** defines the pattern of the support material and raft

   ❑   **Pattern spacing** determines how big that pattern layout is

   ❑   **Pattern angle** will change the way the pattern is drawn in reference to the bed

The two options for **Interface Layers** and **Interface Pattern Spacing** are for the layers between the raft and the model. Having these layers will help us to remove the raft from the model after it is done printing. Depending on the plastic, the printer, and of course the model, these settings will need some experimentation to dial in. Once they are through, they will allow for easy removal of the raft, sometimes as easy as peeling it away with our fingers.

Changing Cooling settings

1. Click on the **Filament Settings** tab.

2. Select the **Cooling** option from the left-hand side menu. You can see that the options for the printer's cooling fan are laid out.

   Cooling in our type of printing is crucial in making sure prints don't warp or crack from too much or too little cooling

3. A good place to start tweaking the cooling settings is the **Disable fan for the first X layers** option. Laying down several layers before cooling will help prevent the model from warping up off the bed before more layers are in place to hold its shape.

How it works...

Now that we know how to change the settings here and little of what they do, let's go over things in a bit more detail. First, let's look at the changes we made in the **Print Settings** tab.

1. First, let us look at **Infill** settings:

   ❑ We talked about what the different infill settings can do, such as making parts more structurally sound. We didn't talk about what infill actually is. **Infill** is the fill inside of an object that we print. Using a lot of plastic inside our prints is not only a waste, because we'll never see it, but it also makes our print times extraordinarily high.

   ❑ So we have to take our infill settings seriously. For objects that are hollow or nearly hollow, less infill is good. If the upper layers are dome-like, we'll need a higher infill setting. Also, if our parts are for, say, a new 3D printer we are building, we'll want our infill settings higher as well so the parts can take the strain.

   ❑ One interesting thing to try is to make a simple model—a square or a circle. Then set the infill pattern to **honeycomb** and when printing it, print it without a raft and set it to have 0 top and bottom layers. The resulting print will look a lot like an air filter grill for a computer or other electronics projects. Useful.

2. Now we'll have a look at the **Speed** settings:

   ❑ This is where we can get a lot of tweaking done. Speed settings control the speed of almost every aspect of the printing process. There are a lot of settings here. So set the layer height to be thicker as we talked about previously, and then we can see where the problems in our print occur because of speed.

   ❑ Almost always, the speed errors will be regarding the movement of the printer being too fast. With the settings available to us though, it is possible to slow down the printer at just the points that it is having trouble, while not slowing down the whole printing process.

3. The **Skirt** and **Brim** settings are next, to prevent our models from warping or popping off the bed:

- So the skirt of the printing is the line of filament that is extruded onto the bed around the object. The main reason for it is to ensure that the hot end is at the correct temperature and the filament is flowing before the printer gets to the actual object. Some printers may take longer to come up to temperature, especially with some plastics; so adjusting the number of loops and the skirt height may be needed to make sure the printer is ready, giving us a chance to stop it early if it is not.

- The brim settings are a bit different. They attach a thin layer of plastic all around the base of the object—a brim. A good way to visualize this is imagining a top hat sitting on a table. The brim of the hat is like the brim we print, surrounding the cylinder of the hat itself. The brim helps the model stick to the bed of the printer. So models with thin areas of the base may need a brim printed on them that will then be removed after the model is done printing.

4. The **Support material** settings prevent overhanging geometry from sagging:

- Support material is used to fill in areas underneath overhangs or other areas that are freestanding. These areas would sag and droop if they didn't have some sort of support. If the model we are printing has overhangs, we'll need support material. The settings here can be tailored to print or not print support material based on the amount of overhang the model has.

- The other thing under the **Support material** settings is the setting for printing a raft. A **raft** is similar to a brim, but it is printed under the entire model. It helps in two ways (if we need it): it keeps the model sticking to the print bed and helps prevent the model from warping as it prints.

- The thing to consider about both support material and rafts are that they will both need to be removed after the print is complete. For rafts, that usually means just peeling it off of the bottom of the model. For support material, we might need to pull out the hobby knives and trim it away.

5. Finally, we will take a look at the **Cooling** settings, so that we don't cool too fast, or too slow:

- Cooling settings can be found under **Filament Settings**. If our printer doesn't have a cooling fan, we don't need to touch these settings. Most printers now though do have a cooling fan to help prevent blobbing and warping of the print.

- The cooling fan speed can be controlled, giving it a base speed range, if we want auto cooling or want to have the fan always on. It can be further controlled by having Slic3r determine if a layer print time is within a certain threshold and either turn the fan on or off for that layer. When printing bridges to span gaps, the default is to have the fan on full so that it will cool the bridging filament to prevent sagging as the bridges are printed.

There's more...

By digging deeper into Slic3r's settings, we will find a variety of settings that we haven't touched on yet. Some we may never use, but some may be important to our specific printer. Here are two examples.

Multiple extruders

Some of us are diving into the deep end and using two or more extruders. Slic3r handles multiple extruders as well. We can find the base settings for multiple extruders under the **Print Settings** tab. Right now, Slic3r is set up so that with these base settings we can have one extruder print our perimeters, another one print infill, and yet a third print support material if we want, and have that all those extruders at our disposal. By default, they are all set to extruder number 1. Those in that deep end can work with those settings to print in multiple types of plastic and even print with dissolvable support material for truly fine prints.

Vibration

Under **Printer Settings**, there is an experimental option for **Vibration**. Depending on the design of the printer, when the print head moves, it is possible to set up a resonance in the printer, causing it to vibrate. As we know, a solid and steady printer is needed for good prints. Setting a value in this preference will cause the printing to slow down if the printer is getting near the vibration frequency. This isn't needed for most printers, but if the printer we are printing on has some wobble, it's a setting worth checking out.

Troubleshooting your prints (Should know)

Home 3D printing is a new field. Your first prints won't be perfect, but with time, and some help here, we can make them better.

Getting ready

Remember those models we used to test our printer capabilities earlier? Well, dig out those files again, because we're going to use them to help troubleshoot our printer problems. If you've gotten rid of those early files, here they are again:

- ▸ Snake by Zomboe (`http://www.thingiverse.com/thing:4743`)
- ▸ Torture Test by MAKE (`http://www.thingiverse.com/thing:33902`)

The following section contains several troubleshooting methods to help with various issues with printing. It will help us go through our Slic3r settings to alleviate or even remove the problems.

How to do it...

One very common problem people have with their printer is the print not sticking to the print bed. There are several possible reasons for this:

- ▶ Check that you've prepared your bed properly. You can do that with either of the following methods:
  - ❑ Using painter's tape
  - ❑ Coating the bed with an ABS slurry (for ABS prints)
  - ❑ Using other mediums to allow the filament to adhere to the bed (certain hairsprays have been used for this purpose)

- ▶ Check that your bed is leveled and that no matter where the hot end is over the bed, the distance between the hot end and the bed is the same.

  To check that distance, slide a piece of paper between bed and hot end. If the paper slides with just a bit of resistance, this is a good distance. If any of the locations you test stick or move to easily, re-level that portion of your bed.

- ▶ Check to see that the bed temperature is hot enough for the first few layers.

  If the bed temperature is too low, the filament will cool too quickly to stick properly.

  Some models are just too thin on the bottom to stay still on the bed. In this case, add in a brim when slicing the model so that the model has more area against the bed to stick.

- ▶ Another common problem is gaps in areas of our prints. There are several steps we can do to reduce or eliminate those gaps:
  - ❑ Check our speed settings for the model and what area it is building
  - ❑ Reduce the layer height of the slices
  - ❑ Make sure the print isn't cooling too much between the layers
  - ❑ If the fan speed is too high, the previous layer may be too cold for the next layer to adhere properly
  - ❑ If the model has a large surface area, the model may cool before the hot end gets back around to putting on a new layer

- ▶ An exceptionally common problem of newly set up printers is print warping. There are a large variety of reasons why warping happens, so let's eliminate the biggest reasons:
  - ❑ Check that the model isn't getting too cold while printing
  - ❑ Keep the print area warm by eliminating drafts around the printer

- ❑ Reduce the speed of the fan during the start of the printing process
- ❑ Make sure our heated bed is staying warm during the printing
- ❑ Check that thin model sections have support
- ❑ Adding support material to the object can help with thin sections
- ❑ Adding a brim can help for thin sections at the base of the model

▸ Sometimes a print will get popped off of the bed during the print. This is usually caused by the hot end hitting the model, but we'll look at another possible cause as well:

- ❑ Check that the printer itself isn't warping or twisted. If the printer structure isn't stable and straight, then the hot end can hit the model, ruining the print or popping it off of the bed.
- ❑ Check that the bed isn't cooling during the print and warping up from the base.

▸ If our hot end is too cold, the filament will not flow properly. This causes stuttering in the filament flow, or dots of filament being extruded instead of a nice clean line.

- ❑ Check to make sure the hot end stays at a consistent temperature
- ❑ Raise the temperature by 10 degrees at a time until the problem stops, and then bring the temperature back down until a good filament flow is reached

▸ Different plastics do not print the same. ABS and PLA print at different temperatures, but different colors of the same plastic type may also require different temperatures.

- ❑ Check the hot end temperature for the filament being printed
- ❑ Look up the recommended temperature for the type of plastic that we are printing
- ❑ If we just changed colors, adjust the temperature up or down based on the symptoms we are seeing
- ❑ If the layers are not adhering or you see a stuttered filament, raise the temperature
- ❑ Reduce the temperature if there is too much squeeze out or the layers are sagging

▸ Sagging of the top layers of a model happens when there are large gaps to cover at the top of the model.

- ❑ Increase our fan speed at the top layers. This will allow the filament to cool more quickly and prevent some sagging.
- ❑ Increase the number of top layers to be printed at the top of the model. Doing this will give more structure to the top layers. The multiple layers will bind together to reduce sagging.

❏ Change the bridging settings in Slic3r to print bridges faster. Bridging settings are in the **Speed** settings in expert preferences

❏ Increase the density or shape of the infill settings.

❏ Very large gaps will need support, and increasing infill will help prevent the top layers from sagging.

How it works...

Troubleshooting is a skill in itself. Many people believe they are troubleshooting, when really they are causing more problems for themselves by fiddling and changing things, but not paying close attention to what they are actually doing. If it works for them, they are satisfied.

Unfortunately, those people are missing half of what troubleshooting is about—learning more about the thing they are working on.

We've talked before about changing one setting at a time in this book. There's a reason for that. Proceeding in a manner that is known will lead us to learn what is actually wrong with our printing, and also show us what changing our settings actually does to our prints.

So many people change settings, fiddle, and look up information that they don't take the time, or don't know how, to troubleshoot. We know the problem, what we are trying to do is find the cause. We can't find the cause if we don't approach our troubleshooting with a plan in mind.

▶ **Check all of our settings**: Make sure we loaded the right configuration file for our plastic and model.

▶ **Check our printer**: Is it still stable and calibrated?

▶ **Start with the most likely settings, and change only one setting at a time**: Changing more than one setting might make the problem worse, or appear to fix it but actually mask the real issue. Worse, we could introduce a new problem while fixing the old, which would lead to loss in time and plastic.

These steps are very simple, but essential for us to remember when trying to solve issues with our printing. Taking small steps and noting the changes will help us understand our printer's capabilities better, and help us diagnose problems more quickly in the future.

There's more...

3D printing for us is very new. There are so many things that can go wrong. When something does, try to isolate the issue. Make one change at a time and see how it affects the print. Changing multiple things at the same time to fix an issue won't tell us what worked and what did not, or even what made it worse.

It will take longer to solve with this method. When we run into the same issue again in future, and we will, we will remember our earlier issue and have a good place to start when troubleshooting the new one.

Running Slic3r from the command line (Become an expert)

Some of us like our GUIs, but some of us yearn for the control and options that only the command line can give. The creators of Slic3r are our kind of people. They've built in command line usage into Slic3r from the early stages of the project.

So far we have created prints from the graphical interface. Slic3r can also be controlled and tweaked from the command line, which gives the user more power and control over the printing process.

Getting ready

So now that we know about the command line, how do we get to it?

- ▶ Windows:
    1. Open a command window and navigate to the directory where we uncompressed Slic3r.
    2. At the command prompt type `slic3r-console.exe`.

- ▶ Mac:
    1. Open a terminal window and navigate to the directory where Slic3r is installed.
    2. At the prompt type `slic3r.pl -help`.

- ▶ Linux:
    1. Open a terminal window and navigate to the directory where Slic3r is installed.
    2. At the prompt type `slic3r.pl -help`.

We'll now see the list of Slic3r commands that are available to us. If you'd like to look at the list, they are listed in the *How it works...* section of this recipe.

One caveat for these instructions: As of the time of this writing, the Windows version of `slic3r-console` has a bug in it. We can substitute `slic3r.exe` to slice from the command line, but it will not have any console output.

How to do it...

Because Slic3r command line options are normally built in one line, we'll be splitting out the options into separate steps. At the end, we'll put it all together to run.

 The Windows command is different from the Mac and Linux version. We'll be demonstrating the Linux and Mac command, just substitute `slicer-console` in for `slicer.pl`.

1. Load in our current configuration using the following command:

   `slicer.pl --load <config filename>`

2. Add in our options. In this case, changing the size of our object to twice the size:

   `--scale 2`

3. Finally, we give Slic3r the name of our model:

   `<modelFilename.stl>`

Slic3r will take the file, scale it up 200 percent as it slices it, and then output our file to `modelFilename.gcode`.

 This method could be used to automate our printing process, batch slice a variety of files, and even process one file for a multitude of printer configurations.

How it works...

So now that we've looked at some things we can do with the command-line options, the ideas for what else we can do are starting to come to mind. The command-line options can be called from the programs we write, or set up to run later using the scheduling in Windows or cron on Linux and Mac. We can also set up web pages or mobile apps to call Slic3r.

The following is a list of what we see when we list out the help for Slic3r. There are wealth of options available to us. Look through it, and ideas for how to use Slic3r from the command line will continue to flow:

```
Slic3r 0.9.10b is a STL-to-GCODE translator for RepRap 3D printers
written by Alessandro Ranellucci <aar@cpan.org> - http://slic3r.org/

Usage: slic3r.pl [ OPTIONS ] file.stl
```

This first section of the help is the general options, allowing us to check the version, to load and save configuration files, and even specify the number of processor threads that Slic3r can use. The following table lists them out:

`--help`	Outputs this usage screen and exits
`--version`	Outputs the version of Slic3r and exits
`--save <file>`	Saves the configuration to the specified file
`--load <file>`	Load the configuration from the specified file. It can be used more than once to load options from multiple files.
`-o, --output <file>`	File to output G-code to (by default, the file will be saved into the same directory as the input file using the `--output-filename-` format to generate the filename)
`-j, --threads <num>`	Number of threads to use (1+, default: 2)

The output options are exactly what it says, the different settings we can use for output. This includes post processing, svg export, and merging multiple files into a single print.

Output option:	
`--output-filename-format`	The output filename format; all config options enclosed in brackets will be replaced by their values, as well as `[input_filename_base]` and `[input_filename]` (default: `[input_filename_base].gcode`)
`--post-process`	Generated G-code will be processed with the supplied script; call this more than once to process through multiple scripts.
`--export-svg`	Export a SVG file containing slices instead of G-code.
`-m, --merge`	If multiple files are supplied, they will be composed into a single print rather than processed individually.

Here is where we can tell Slic3r about our printer: the physical sizes, and what type of G-code that Slic3r should expect.

Printer options	
`--nozzle-diameter`	Diameter of nozzle in mm (default: `0.5`)
`--print-center`	Coordinates in mm of the point to center the print around (default: `100,100`)
`--z-offset`	Additional height in mm to add to vertical coordinates (+/-, default: `0`)

Printer options	
`--gcode-flavor`	The type of G-code to generate (`reprap`/`teacup`/`makerbot`/`sailfish`/`mach3`/`no-extrusion`, default: `recprap`)
`--use-relative-e-distances`	Enable this to get relative E values
`--gcode-arcs`	Use G2/G3 commands for native arcs (experimental, not supported by all firmware)
`--g0`	Use G0 commands for retraction (experimental, not supported by all firmware)
`--gcode-comments`	Make G-code verbose by adding comments (default: `no`)
`--vibration-limit`	Limit the frequency of moves on X and Y axes (Hz, set zero to disable; default: `0`)

Filament options gives us finer control over how Slic3r will handle our plastic that we are printing with. We can change the first layer's temperature compared to the later layers, what the bed temperature should be, and what diameter filament we are using.

Filament option	
`--filament-diameter`	Diameter in mm of your raw filament (default: `3`)
`--extrusion-multiplier`	Change this to alter the amount of plastic extruded. There should be very little need to change this value, which is only useful to compensate for filament packing (default: `1`)
`--temperature`	Extrusion temperature in degree Celsius; set 0 to disable (default: `200`)
`--first-layer-temperature`	Extrusion temperature for the first layer in degree Celsius; set 0 to disable (default: same as `--temperature`)
`--bed-temperature`	Heated bed temperature in degree Celsius; set 0 to disable (default: `0`)
`--first-layer-bed-temperature`	Heated bed temperature for the first layer, in degree Celsius, set 0 to disable (default: same as `--bed-temperature`)

Speed options is where we can make our prints run faster, but if we aren't careful we will sacrifice quality. Some areas, such as gap filling, we may want to run faster, so there is less chance of sagging.

Speed options	
`--travel-speed`	Speed of non-print moves in mm/s (default: 130)
`--perimeter-speed`	Speed of print moves for perimeters in mm/s (default: 30)
`--small-perimeter-speed`	Speed of print moves for small perimeters in mm/s or % over perimeter speed (default: 30)
`--external-perimeter-speed`	Speed of print moves for the external perimeter in mm/s or % over perimeter speed (default: 70)
`--infill-speed`	Speed of print moves in mm/s (default: 60)
`--solid-infill-speed`	Speed of print moves for solid surfaces in mm/s or % over infill speed (default: 60)
`--top-solid-infill-speed`	Speed of print moves for top surfaces in mm/s or % over solid infill speed (default: 50)
`--support-material-speed`	Speed of support material print moves in mm/s (default: 60)
`--bridge-speed`	Speed of bridge print moves in mm/s (default: 60)
`--gap-fill-speed`	Speed of gap fill print moves in mm/s (default: 20)
`--first-layer-speed`	Speed of print moves for bottom layer, expressed either as an absolute value or as a percentage over normal speeds (default: 30%)

Depending on the physical stability of our printer, adding in acceleration with these options can help speed up and improve the quality of our print.

Acceleration options	
`--perimeter-acceleration`	Overrides firmware's default acceleration for perimeters. (mm/s^2, set zero to disable; default: 0)
`--infill-acceleration`	Overrides firmware's default acceleration for infill. (mm/s^2, set zero to disable; default: 0)
`--default-acceleration`	Acceleration will be reset to this value after the specific settings have been applied. (mm/s^2, set zero to disable; default: 130)

Accuracy options is a little misleading. While adjusting layer height does usually yield smoother prints, adding in infill can also make the print sturdier.

Accuracy options	
`--layer-height`	Layer height in mm (default: 0.4)
`--first-layer-height`	Layer height for first layer (mm or %, default: 0.35)
`--infill-every-layers`	Infill every *N* layers (default: 1)
`--solid-infill-every-layers`	Force a solid layer every *N* layers (default: 0)

Print options is also confusing at first, because it sounds like a catch-all category. These are the actual settings for the object to be printed: if it should have a solid top or bottom, how dense the fill material will be, and also allow us to use custom G-code for the start and end of the print.

Print options	
`--perimeters`	Number of perimeters/horizontal skins (range: 0+, default: 3)
`--top-solid-layers`	Number of solid layers to be done for top surfaces (range: 0+, default: 3)
`--bottom-solid-layers`	Number of solid layers to be done for bottom surfaces (range: 0+, default: 3)
`--solid-layers`	Shortcut for setting the preceding two options at once
`--fill-density`	Infill density (range: 0-1, default: 0.4)
`--fill-angle`	Infill angle in degrees (range: 0-90, default: 45)
`--fill-pattern`	Pattern to use to fill non-solid layers (default: honeycomb)
`--solid-fill-pattern`	Pattern to use to fill solid layers (default: rectilinear)
`--start-gcode`	Load the initial G-code from the supplied file. This will overwrite the default command (home all axes [G28]).
`--end-gcode`	Load the final G-code from the supplied file. This will overwrite the default commands (turn off temperature [M104 S0], home X axis [G28 X], disable motors [M84]).
`--layer-gcode`	Load `layer-change` G-code from the supplied file (default: nothing).
`--toolchange-gcode`	Load `tool-change` G-code from the supplied file (default: nothing).

Print options	
`--extra-perimeters`	Add more perimeters when needed (default: `yes`)
`--randomize-start`	Randomize the starting point across layers (default: `yes`)
`--only-retract-when-crossing-perimeters`	Disable retraction when travelling between infill paths inside the same island (default: `no`)
`--solid-infill-below-area`	Force solid infill when a region has a smaller area than the current threshold (mm^2, default: `70`)

When we use support material, the following are the settings we would want to adjust. These tell Slic3r to use a support material or not, and where.

Support material options	
`--support-material`	Generate support material for overhangs
`--support-material-threshold`	Overhang threshold angle (range: 0-90, set 0 for automatic detection, default: `0`)
`--support-material-pattern`	Pattern to use for support material (default: `rectilinear`)
`--support-material-spacing`	Spacing between pattern lines (mm, default: `2.5`)
`--support-material-angle`	Support material angle in degrees (range: 0-90, default: `0`)

Since the extruder is making the plastic filament more liquid, we will sometimes need the extruder to run backward, pulling the plastic back in so we don't get blobbing and dripping.

Retraction option	
`--retract-length`	Length of retraction in mm when pausing extrusion (default: `1`)
`--retract-speed`	Speed for retraction in mm/s (default: `30`)
`--retract-restart-extra`	Additional amount of filament in mm to push after compensating retraction (default: `0`)
`--retract-before-travel`	Only retract-before-travel moves of this length in mm (default: `2`)
`--retract-lift`	Lift Z by the given distance in mm when retracting (default: `0`)

If we are using multiple extruders, we definitely want to retract the plastic of the extruder that just finished so that it doesn't drip or dribble over the new plastic from the other extruder.

Retraction options for multi-extruder setups	
`--retract-length-toolchange`	Length of retraction in mm when disabling tool (default: 1)
`--retract-restart-extra-toolchange`	Additional amount of filament in mm to push after switching tool (default: 0)

Having the print sag, pop off the build platform and having gaps between layers can all be related to improper cooling. Slic3r gives us good controls over the cooling of the print with the following settings:

Cooling options	
`--cooling`	Enable fan and cooling control
`--min-fan-speed`	Minimum fan speed (default: 35%)
`--max-fan-speed`	Maximum fan speed (default: 100%)
`--bridge-fan-speed`	Fan speed to use when bridging (default: 100%)
`--fan-below-layer-time`	Enable fan if layer print time is below this approximate number of seconds (default: 60)
`--slowdown-below-layer-time`	Slow down if layer print time is below this approximate number of seconds (default: 30)
`--min-print-speed`	Minimum print speed (mm/s, default: 10)
`--disable-fan-first-layers`	Disable fan for the first *N* layers (default: 1)
`--fan-always-on`	Keep fan always on at min fan speed, even for layers that don't need cooling

If we need to pre-extrude some plastic before printing the object, or have Slic3r add a brim to help the model stick to the platform, the following are the settings we will use.

Skirt options	
`--skirts`	Number of skirts to draw (0+, default: 1)
`--skirt-distance`	Distance in mm between the innermost skirt and the object (default: 6)
`--skirt-height`	Height of skirts to draw (expressed in layers, 0+, default: 1)

Skirt options	
`--min-skirt-length`	Generate no less than the number of loops required to consume this length of filament on the first layer, for each extruder (mm, 0+, default: 0)
`--brim-width`	Width of the brim that will get added to each object to help adhesion (mm, default: 0)

We can change the size and position of the object we want to print, without going back to edit the model. Using the two duplicate settings, we can even print several copies of the same object at the same time.

Transform options	
`--scale`	Factor for scaling input object (default: 1)
`--rotate`	Rotation angle in degrees (0-360, default: 0)
`--duplicate`	Number of items with auto-arrange (1+, default: 1)
`--bed-size`	Bed size, only used for auto-arrange (mm, default: 200,200)
`--duplicate-grid`	Number of items with grid arrangement (default: 1,1)
`--duplicate-distance`	Distance in mm between copies (default: 6)

Sometimes we want to finish a whole object in a print file before moving on to the next one in the file. We need to be careful about where the extruder head goes so that it doesn't hit any of the objects. Also, having one of the parts done while the others print can sometimes be just what we need.

Sequential printing options	
`--complete-objects`	When printing multiple objects and/or copies, complete each one before starting the next one; watch out for extruder collisions (default: no)
`--extruder-clearance-radius`	Radius in mm above which the extruder won't collide with anything (default: 20)
`--extruder-clearance-height`	Maximum vertical extruder depth; that is, the vertical distance from the extruder tip and carriage bottom (default: 20)

If we want to add in some comments to the output file, such as the date it was printed, what printer settings were used, even notes to ourselves on why we used the settings we did, we can put those in using the following option:

Miscellaneous options	
`--notes`	Notes to be added as comments to the output file

The following are fairly advanced options, dealing with how wide the Slic3r will make the extrusion layer, if it should have a different first layer, and even have a different width between the perimeter and infill:

Flow options (advanced)	
`--extrusion-width`	Set the extrusion width manually; it accepts either an absolute value in mm (such as `0.65`) or a percentage over layer height (such as `200%`)
`--first-layer-extrusion-width`	Set a different extrusion width for the first layer
`--perimeter-extrusion-width`	Set a different extrusion width for perimeters
`--infill-extrusion-width`	Set a different extrusion width for infill
`--support-material-extrusion-width`	Set a different extrusion width for support material
`--bridge-flow-ratio`	Multiplier for extrusion when bridging (> 0, default: `1`)

Previously, we had some multi-extruder options with the retraction settings. These settings round out the other settings that we need to use with more than one extruder.

Multiple extruder options	
`--extruder-offset`	Offset of each extruder, if firmware doesn't handle the displacement (can be specified multiple times, default: `0x0`)
`--perimeter-extruder`	Extruder to use for perimeters (1+, default: 1)
`--infill-extruder`	Extruder to use for infill (1+, default: 1)
`--support-material-extruder`	Extruder to use for support material (1+, default: 1)

There's more...

There are many things that we can do with access to the command line. Every system that it runs on is capable of running a timed process, or a batch process.

So let's think about a few things we could do by using the command line. We could make a process that accepts models from the Web and automatically slices them and start a print remotely. We could even set up a webcam to watch the print in progress.

Taking that one step further, we could have other people upload their models. A Slic3r script could then calculate the amount of plastic needed and charge them for the print. They could watch the print on the webcam and see the results even before we put it in the mail to deliver.

That's just one idea of what we could do with access to the command line. Just like having your own 3D printer at your disposal, the sky is the limit for what we can do with Slic3r.

The basics of G-code (Should know)

We've talked about G-code at various points in this book. We know that it's the code that Slic3r produces and sends to the printer. What exactly is it though? How can we alter it directly to affect our prints? In this recipe, we'll look at a model sliced by Slic3r in order to better understand how our printer functions.

Getting ready

For this recipe, let's slice up one of our torture test files to look at. Let's take Snake by Zomboe (`http://www.thingiverse.com/thing:4743`) to look at.

We will slice the file and take a look at the generated G-code that Slic3r produces.

How to do it...

1. Load up Slic3r. For this example, we will use its GUI.

2. In the **Output options** on the **Print Settings** tab, check the box with **Verbose G-code**. We do this to get more information on what our G-code is doing, it turns on comments for all of the lines of G-code:

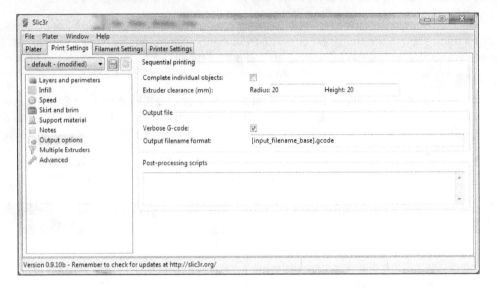

3. Slice our model, taking note where we saved it.

4. Open the sliced model into a text editor. The sliced model will be named `<filename>.gcode`.

How it works...

Now that we have our model sliced, let's take a look at it:

```
; generated by Slic3r 0.9.10b on 2013-08-07 at 08:28:44

; layer_height = 0.4
; perimeters = 3
; top_solid_layers = 3
; bottom_solid_layers = 3
; fill_density = 0.4
; perimeter_speed = 30
; infill_speed = 60
; travel_speed = 130
; nozzle_diameter = 0.5
; filament_diameter = 3
; extrusion_multiplier = 1
; perimeters extrusion width = 0.53mm
```

```
; infill extrusion width = 0.53mm
; solid infill extrusion width = 0.53mm
; top infill extrusion width = 0.53mm
; first layer extrusion width = 0.70mm

G21 ; set units to millimeters
M107 ; disable fan
M104 S200 ; set temperature
G28 ; home all axes
G1 Z5 F5000 ; lift nozzle

M109 S200 ; wait for temperature to be reached
G90 ; use absolute coordinates
G92 E0 ; reset extrusion distance
M82 ; use absolute distances for extrusion
G1 F1800.000 E-1.00000 ; retract
G92 E0 ; reset extrusion distance
G1 Z0.350 F7800.000 ; move to next layer (0)
G1 X55.204 Y56.037 ; move to first skirt point
G1 F1800.000 E1.00000 ; compensate retraction
G1 X56.044 Y55.197 F540.000 E1.03865 ; skirt
G1 X57.054 Y54.367 E1.08118 ; skirt
G1 X58.204 Y53.757 E1.12354 ; skirt
.
. <truncated for brevity>
.
G1 X114.772 Y113.057 F600.000 E1.01138 ; perimeter
G1 F1800.000 E0.01138 ; retract
G92 E0 ; reset extrusion distance
M107 ; disable fan
M104 S0 ; turn off temperature
G28 X0  ; home X axis
M84     ; disable motors

; filament used = 681.3mm (4.8cm3)

; avoid_crossing_perimeters = 0
; bed_size = 200,200
; bed_temperature = 0
.
. <truncated for brevity>
.
; wipe = 0
; z_offset = 0
```

The actual file is much longer than the one we have here, but this gives us a good section to look at. So what are we seeing here?

The first part, each line starting with a semi-colon (;) are comments. They tell us when the file was slice, and helpfully, what are the settings for. So if we have a file that we feel prints perfectly, but don't know what configuration we used, we can go back to the sliced file and get the settings again.

The settings at the bottom of the sliced file are only available with Verbose G-code. The settings at the top of the file are there in normal mode.

In G-code, the semi-colon (;) stands for a comment. Comments can be on a line by themselves or as part of a line:

```
; first layer extrusion width = 0.70mm
M104 S0 ; turn off temperature
```

Once a comment is started though, it continues to the end of the line. This may be useful if we want to save a sliced file and add in notes of our own. We can also use post-processing scripts to add in G-code, and comments about what it does.

After the comments is a long set of lines with letters and numbers. The letters indicate the type of action that is to be performed, and the numbers indicate either the action itself, or the interval that is used in the action.

More information on 3D printing G-code can be found at the RepRap wiki (http://reprap. org/wiki/G-code). Though not all firmware support all of the G-codes listed there.

The following list contains the most common letters in our G-code file. They are listed in order of importance and frequency:

- ▶ G: Prepares the machine for movement and the type of movement wanted.
- ▶ M: In G-code M is an auxiliary function; in our case telling our printer to do something specific to 3D printing. This controls the heated bed, fan, extruder, and other 3D printing-specific mechanical parts.
- ▶ X, Y, and Z: These are for the location that the nozzle should go to at that point in the G-code. We will usually see X and Y together, with Z added when the hot end is raised or bed lowered, depending on our printer style.
- ▶ F: This is for the feed rate of our filament.
- ▶ E: Defines the precision for our feed rate. When coupled with F, it defines how our filament is extruded. A negative number means our filament is being extracted to prevent blobbing or threads of filament.
- ▶ S: In most G-code it defines the speed of the tool. When it is coupled with a code responsible for temperature, it defines the temperature for that part.

There's more...

Slic3r also allows us to input extra G-code at the time of slicing. We can have it input code at the start of a print, the end of a print, each time a print layer is finished, and whenever a tool is changed (in our case, this means switching to a different extruder).

 Custom starting G-code commands are inserted after the temperature control codes for the heated bed and extruder.

These can be set in the **Printer Settings** tab under the **Custom G-code** selection. We see that Slic3r already puts in some G-code for us for the common printing tasks.

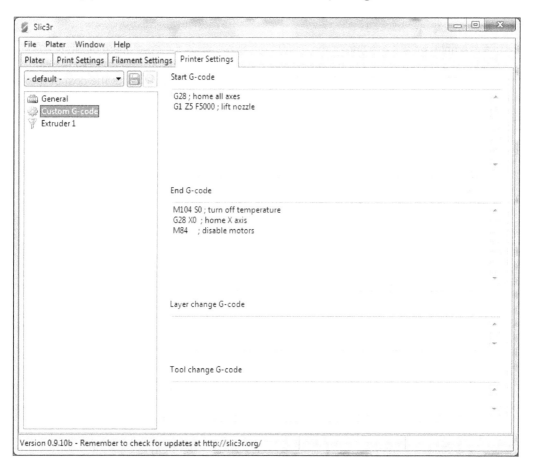

Post processing with Slic3r (Become an expert)

Our models aren't always perfect. Sometimes when we slice a model, there are issues with interpreting its geometry. Sometimes we just want to play around with the G-code to see how it will affect the model and print. That is where post processing comes in.

We can set up Slic3r to automatically run a post-processing script on our sliced model. Post-processing scripts can do things such as removing stray lines from the model to reducing the chance of blobbing on some surfaces; or even calculating the weight of filament that is needed to produce the model and give us the cost for that model in materials.

Getting ready

For this example, we will use one of the scripts put together by the developers of Slic3r to compute the cost of the filament used. The example script is in Euros, and the cost is just an example. To get the cost, we will need to change the units later, calculate the cost of the filament we are actually using, and put it into the script. For now though, we will go with the default script.

 For Windows users, the current post-processing scripts are written in Perl. Users will need to install Perl in order to run these post-processing scripts.

How to do it...

1. Get the `filament-weight.pl` script from the Slic3r GitHub at `https://github.com/alexrj/Slic3r/tree/master/utils/post-processing`.

2. In the **Print Settings** tab, select **Output options**.

3. In the **Post-processing scripts** section, input the absolute path to the script we are running. For example, on Windows, use `C:\Slic3r\scripts\filament-weight.pl`.

4. Slice the file. In this case we are using the Snake example again.

5. Once the slicing is finished and if we open the file, we will find the following at the end of the file:

```
; filament used = 681.3mm (4.8cm3 or 6.00g PLA/5.04g ABS)
; costs = EUR 0.30 (PLA), EUR 0.10 (ABS)
```

This is different from the original G-code file ending of:

```
;  filament used = 681.3mm (4.8cm3)
```

If using a Windows machine gives an error, or the output G-code file does not change when the post-processing script is run, a change has to be made to the post-processing script.

Windows machines have limitations on how many processes can access a file at the same time. To get around this, we can make a backup file of the original and then run our process on the original. To do this we add `$^I = '.bak';` before the `While` loop in the PERL script.

There's more...

A good idea is to keep all of our scripts in one place. A `scripts` folder inside the Slic3r folder is a good place, or you can place it in our user directory. When updating Slic3r, make sure that we back up the folder before installing the new version.

Each script must be executable by the host system, and must be a script that the host system can run. As noted previously, Perl isn't on Windows by default, so it would need to be installed. However, other scripting languages could be used by Slic3r.

Post processing scripts are passed the full path to the sliced file. Slic3r configuration options are available to post-processing scripts as environment variables that start with `SLIC3R_`.

Because post-processing scripts are able to call anything they normally could, it is even possible to make calls to a server and pass along data for the server to store or do other things with.

As mentioned in the previous section, the scripts don't have to be all in Perl. It just happens to be the language that the developers prefer, and that Slic3r itself is written in.

For Linux and Mac users, we can use shell scripts to call other programs, or do processing itself.

For Windows users, the basic batch file can be called.

If we need arguments passed to the script, Slic3r cannot do that. We would need to create another script for Slic3r that wraps our original script. That script would then call our original script with the arguments we want.

Thank you for buying
Instant Slic3r

About Packt Publishing

Packt, pronounced 'packed', published its first book "*Mastering phpMyAdmin for Effective MySQL Management*" in April 2004 and subsequently continued to specialize in publishing highly focused books on specific technologies and solutions.

Our books and publications share the experiences of your fellow IT professionals in adapting and customizing today's systems, applications, and frameworks. Our solution based books give you the knowledge and power to customize the software and technologies you're using to get the job done. Packt books are more specific and less general than the IT books you have seen in the past. Our unique business model allows us to bring you more focused information, giving you more of what you need to know, and less of what you don't.

Packt is a modern, yet unique publishing company, which focuses on producing quality, cutting-edge books for communities of developers, administrators, and newbies alike. For more information, please visit our website: www.packtpub.com.

Writing for Packt

We welcome all inquiries from people who are interested in authoring. Book proposals should be sent to author@packtpub.com. If your book idea is still at an early stage and you would like to discuss it first before writing a formal book proposal, contact us; one of our commissioning editors will get in touch with you.

We're not just looking for published authors; if you have strong technical skills but no writing experience, our experienced editors can help you develop a writing career, or simply get some additional reward for your expertise.

3D Printing Blueprints

ISBN: 978-1-84969-708-8   Paperback: 310 pages

Design successful models for home 3D printing, using a Makerbot or other 3D printers

1. Design 3D models that will print successfully using Blender, a free 3D modeling program

2. Customize, edit, repair, and then share your creations on Makerbot's Thingiverse website

3. Easy-to-follow guide on 3D printing; learn to create a new model at the end of each chapter

Processing 2: Creative Coding Hotshot

ISBN: 978-1-78216-672-6   Paperback: 266 pages

Learn Processing with exciting and engaging projects to make your computer talk, hear, express emotions, and even design physical objects

1. Teach your computer to create physical objects, visualize data, and program a custom hardware controller

2. Create projects that can be run on a variety of platforms, ranging from desktop computers to Android smartphones

3. Each chapter presents a complete project and guides you through the implementation using easy-to-follow, step-by-step instructions

Please check **www.PacktPub.com** for information on our titles

Blender 2.6 Cycles: Materials and Textures Cookbook

ISBN: 978-1-78216-130-1   Paperback: 280 pages

Over 40 recipes to help you create stunning materials and textures using the Cycles rendering engine with Blender

1. Create naturalistic materials and textures - such as rock, snow, ice and fire - using Cycles

2. Learn Cycle's node-based material system

3. Get to grips with the powerful Cycles rendering engine

KeyShot 3D Rendering

ISBN: 978-1-84969-482-7   Paperback: 124 pages

Showcase your 3D models and create hyper realistic images with Keyshot in the fastest and most efficient way possible

1. Create professional quality images from your 3D models in just a few steps

2. Thorough overview of how to work and navigate in KeyShot

3. A step-by-step guide that quickly gets you started with creating realistic images

Please check **www.PacktPub.com** for information on our titles